WHAT GOES UP!

Contents

Dee Reid

Story illustrated by
Martin Chatterton

Find out about

- Escalators and lifts

Tricky words

- escalator
- inside
- building
- outside

Introduce these tricky words and help the reader when they come across them later!

Text starter

Escalators and lifts take you up and down. Most escalators and lifts are on the inside of buildings but some are on the outside! Would you like to go on an escalator or lift like that?

Going Up!

Have you ever been on an escalator?

This escalator is on the inside of the building.

It goes up to the top
of the building.

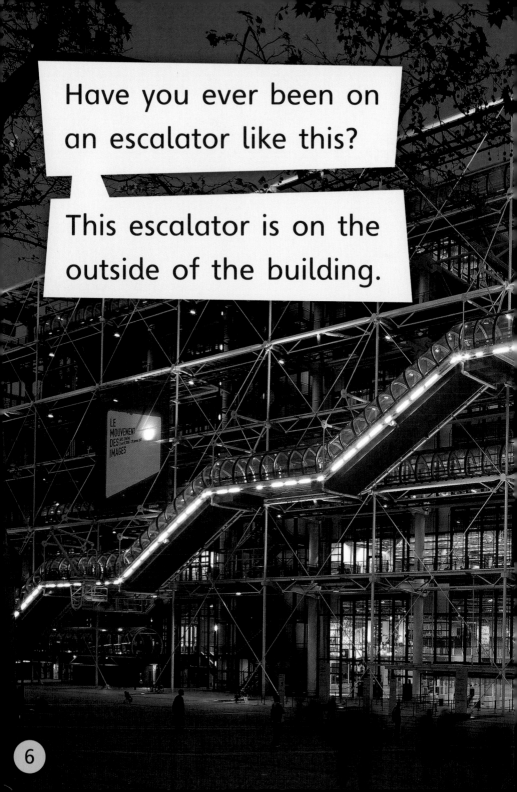

Have you ever been on an escalator like this?

This escalator is on the outside of the building.

6

It goes up very fast.

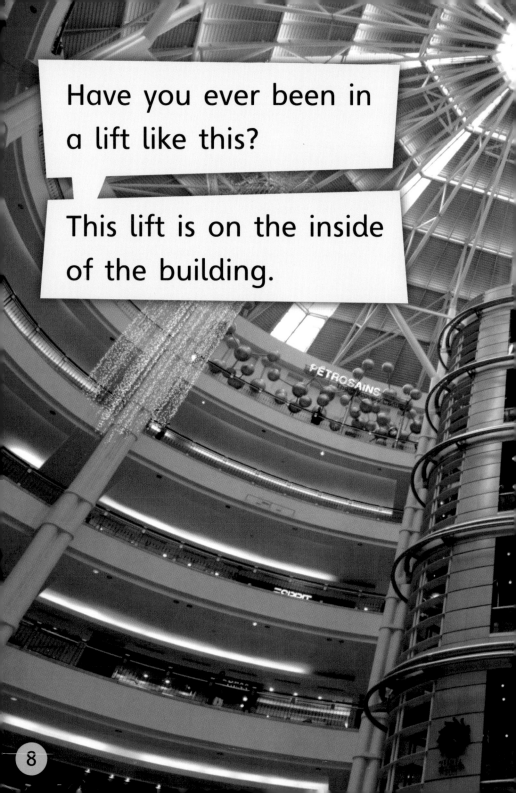

Have you ever been in a lift like this?

This lift is on the inside of the building.

It goes up to the top
of the building.

This lift is on the outside of the building.

It goes up very fast.

Quiz

Text Detective

- Why do we have escalators?
- Do you like going on escalators? Why?

Word Detective

- **Phonic Focus:** Final phonemes

  Page 7: Find a word ending with the phoneme 'p'.
- Page 6: Which sentence is a question? How can you tell?
- Page 9: How many words are there in this sentence?

Super Speller

Read these words:

top   the

Now try to spell them!

HA! HA! HA!

Q What did one lift say to the other?

A I think I'm coming down with something.

11

Before Reading

In this story

Silly Sid

Tricky words

- town
- escalator
- bottom
- meant
- higher

Introduce these tricky words and help the reader when they come across them later!

Story starter

Silly Sid is a bit silly. One day, he went to the town. He saw escalators going up and down. He decided to go on the escalator.

Silly Sid Goes Up and Down

Silly Sid went to the town.

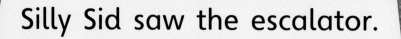

Silly Sid saw the escalator.

"I will go on the escalator," he said.

Silly Sid went down
on the escalator.

At the bottom, he got off.

"I am silly," said Silly Sid. "I meant to go on the UP escalator."

Silly Sid got on the UP escalator.

He went up.

GROUND
FLOOR

"I am silly," said Silly Sid.
"I meant to go up higher."

Silly Sid got on the escalator.

"I am not so silly," said Silly Sid.

Quiz

Text Detective

- Was Silly Sid silly in the end?
- Why is it funny when Silly Sid says, "I am not so silly"?

Word Detective

- **Phonic Focus:** Final phonemes

  Page 16: Find a word ending with the phoneme 'n'.
- Page 14: Find a word with four syllables (beats).
- Page 15: What does Silly Sid actually say?

Super Speller

Read these words:

saw   off

Now try to spell them!

HA! HA! HA!

Q What's black and white and goes up and down?

 A A penguin in a lift.